The Poetry of William Morris

more than it saddens, and is chiefly valued as a proof and portion of repose. To build for us this

> "Shadowy isle of bliss,
> 'Mid most the beating of the steely sea
> Where tossed about all hearts of men must be,"

has been Mr. Morris's work as a poet, and to these pleasures he invites us,—in the pauses of our labor or our warfare,—to rest and forgetfulness and the dreaming of dreams

In an age like this, which has had so much to say about the mission of the poet as a teacher, a thinker, a prophet, an apostle of humanity, and so forth, it may seem strange to some to hear a considerable poet declaring frankly that his chief aim is to give pleasure, but if they will consider how many and various things are included in the giving of pleasure, and will call to mind that the undoubted first object which two of our greatest poets, Chaucer and Shakespeare, had in view, was the amusement of their contemporaries, it need no longer excite surprise But what does excite surprise, and what seems to place Mr Morris in a peculiar position, is the close limitation to which he deliberately commits himself in his choice of subjects and means of treatment Not only does he say to us, my object is simply to amuse you by telling you stories, but he adds also that these stories shall be essentially of only one class, ministering to only one kind of pleasure, and built up of only certain materials to which he confines himself, neglecting or ignoring others, many of them the very ones which we should have expected of a follower of Chaucer, that he would seek out and attempt to use among the very first. And when considering his poems together, we note the effect of this limitation upon them, it is impossible to avoid wishing, perhaps an idle wish, that the poet had either not found it necessary to be content to keep within such bounds, or else that he had more clearly recognized and more zealously guarded against the almost inevitable prolixity and monotony to which writings of such a length attempted under such conditions, must always be most dangerously exposed.

But, except as regards some few, and these generally minor, points of technical treatment, it is idle to lament or blame an artist's limitations. A man can do only his own work, and such limitations as we find in any one's whole work must be regarded for the most part as characteristic and necessary And yet because to know what a man's work is not, is to be on the way to discover what it is, and because Mr. Morris, though too reverent and careful a student of his master to make for himself any claim to be compared with him, is yet professedly the pupil of Chaucer, and has been called by some Chaucerian, it is natural and will probably be useful, to consider in what the two poets are alike and in what respects they differ.

And the truth is that in all essentials the difference between them is so great and so evident that it seems almost absurd to compare them. Chaucer, a man of his age, keenly alive to the political and religious significance of the time; so human, so English, so full of common sense, so social, buoyant, humorous, gay; what has he, so real, so credulous, so confident, so full of faith, in common with the "dreamer of dreams, born out of his due time?" To Chaucer's many sided nature such a philosophy of life as that of Mr. Morris would have been an impossibility, but in Mr Morris it is his very genius, coloring all his work and defining it. Differing from each other so widely as they do in their ideas of life, it is to be expected that this difference should be communicated to their styles. And thus it is The two styles are very different. Read one of Chaucer's tales and then one of Mr. Morris's, and there is seen to be a resemblance, a certain resemblance in the movement of the lines, in the pauses, in the rhymes, and to some extent in the choice of words: but this resemblance is not deep, it is superficial, enough to remind us in a general way of Chaucer, but unfortunately it reminds us also that in Chaucer's style there is a good deal that is not here, we miss the fullness, the variety, the flexibility, the directness, the boldness, the animation, the very life and soul of his verse, and realize that however excellent for his own purposes Mr. Morris's style may be, and however much it may have benefited by his loving study of Chaucer's, its likeness to it is very far from being that of kinship and inheritance A poet who sees so many things, and sees into them so quickly and clearly as Chaucer, who has such various and such deep sympathies, and is so heartily interested in so many and such different persons, must have and cannot help having such a style as Mr Morris neither has nor wants for his expression He has needs for utterance that the other never feels. This is not said in disparagement of Mr. Morris, for, as hereafter will be seen, it is no less true that he too has for his own needs his own fit and admirable expression. What we wish to insist upon is simply that Mr. Morris's style, though formed upon it, is not akin to Chaucer's, and that for the reason that it is merely impossible that two men with such different thoughts about God and man and nature, should have styles resembling each other in any but the most superficial way

Look at their descriptions of scenery and persons Evidently what Mr. Morris, as an artist, regards especially in the master is his objectivity, his love of natural objects for their own sakes; his fondness for the outside of things, for color and form and sound and motion, for things rich and splendid, as well as those that are common and plain, for those qualities, in short, which make a painter of him, a painter whose eye loves rather to dwell upon the object itself than to wander off in search of any moral or spiritual significance which may perhaps be associated with it. But here we wish to call attention to the fact that while Chaucer is almost constantly showing this fondness for the appearances of things, yet in his mention or description of them, it is none the less quite as frequently his characteristic habit to convey with them something more than the things themselves Often in the most delicate and inexplicable way something of his own personality is infused into these descriptions, giving an indescribable charm to the simplest lines, and his eminent skill in the art of making the mention of one thing, without metaphor, the suggestion of another or of many others, is known to all his readers Let us take a few well-known examples, and first, of the way in which his own personal delight in the things he sees and hears enters into his style, and gives a peculiar character to the verse Of birds singing, from the "Cuckow and the Nightingale"—

> "Some songe loude as they had yplained,
> And some in other manner voice yfamed,
> And some all oute with the fulle throte"

How direct the style is here, how full of animation, how glad! and how strong and light and flexible the verse! And now take these well known lines (of which Coleridge is said to have been fond), about sunlit trees in spring —

> ' With branches brode, laden with leves newe
> That sprongen out agen the sunne shene
> Some very redde and some a glad light green "

There is very little description here, but there is a magical something about the verse that brings all the fresh beauty of the scene before us even more vividly perhaps than the actual sight of it could do for most of us. We have not only the scene itself, but Chaucer's delight in it besides. No amount of detail could have given it to us so perfectly and so happily Shakespeare in the great moonlight scene in the "Merchant of Venice," with hardly any, even the slightest description, manages to convey all the unutterable charm of moonlight and the clear, still night to us, by simply bringing us in sympathy with Lorenzo and Jessica, whose souls are steeped in its delight. Of the same kind is Chaucer's brief and simple mention of the nightingale and the moon.

> " A nyghtyngale upon a cedre grene,
> Under the chambre wal ther as she lay,
> Ful lowde song agen the moone shene "

And now see how he speaks of the grass, English grass, as Marsh has noticed —

> ———"the grene grass
> So smale, so thicke, so short, so fresh of hewe "

This is simplicity itself, the simplicity of pure, unreflecting delight. The verse seems to move over the grass in which the poet has such joy as if it were his hand stroking it,—

> "So smale so thicke, so short, so fresh of hewe!"

Again, take this from the "Legende of Goode Women"

> " Upon the smale, softe, swote grass
> That was with flowres swote embrouded al "

Once more, take this for straightforwardness about the flying hart —

> "Ther was the hert y-wont to have his flight,
> And over a brook, and so forth in his weye,"

and this for its fullness and strength,—

> " With knotty knarry bareyn trees olde "

And now take some examples of that other characteristic of Chaucer's style just spoken of, its way of indirectly or covertly suggesting one thing by another. For instance: sailors are proverbially bad riders, and Chaucer says in his direct way of his Schipman, that,

> "He rood upon a rouncy, as he couthe"

He had hired a hackney horse and rode him "as he could." Of the Monk, a full fed, rosy, well-dressed man of the world, fonder of the hunt than of the cloister, he says —

> "And when he rood, men might his bridel heere
> Gyngle in a whistling wind so cleere,
> And eek as lowde as doth the chapel belle,'

implying not only that the monk was a man of fashion, who decorated his horse's bridle with "bells and bosses brave" but hinting good-naturedly also that he had a quicker ear for these than for the chapel bell. And with all this how delightful only for itself is that second line,

> "Gyngle in a whistling wind so cleere!"

In the Sompnoure's tale, a lazy, impudent, begging friar comes into Thomas's house and makes himself at home —

> "And fro the bench he drof away the cat
> And layd adown his potent and his hat,
> And eek his scrip, and set him soft adown"

Another famous passage, without the humor, is that in which he says of the Schipman,

> "Hardy he was and wise to undertake,
> With many a tempest had his berd ben schake"

These are a few convenient examples of Chaucer's large way of dealing with the things he sees and hears, enough however to show that his style is himself and his verse inseparable from the spirit that informs it and makes it move.

And now recall Mr. Morris's way of looking at similar things, and notice the effect upon his style. Passing over his very characteristic *song* of May, take this from the narrative —

> "Now must these men be glad a little while
> That they had lived to see May once more smile
> Upon the earth, wherefore, as men who know
> How fast the bad days and the good days go

> They gathered at the feast   the fair abode
> Wherein they sat, o'erlooked, across the road
> Unhedged green meads, which willowy streams passed through,
> And on that morn, before the fresh May dew
> Had dried upon the sunniest spot of grass,
> From bush to bush did youths and maidens pass
> In raiment meet for May apparelled,
> Gathering the milk-white blossoms and the red;
> And now, with noon long past, and that bright day
> Growing aweary, on the sunny way
> They wandered, crowned with flowers, and loitering,
> And weary, yet were fresh enough to sing
> The carols of the morn, and pensive, still
> Had cast away their doubt of death and ill,
> And flushed with love, no more grew red with shame."

This is a good specimen of Mr. Morris's style when he is describing or narrating generally. And now read a specimen of Chaucer's style, in general description, of a similar scene:—

> "Forgeten had the erthe his pore estate
> Of wynter, that him naked made and mate,
> And with his swerd of colde so sore greved;
> Now hath th'attempre sunne al that releved
> That naked was, and clad yt new agayn.
> The smale foules, of the seson fayn,
> That of the panter and the nette ben scapëd,
> Upon the foweler, that hem made awhapëd
> In winter, and distroyed hadde hire broode,
> In his dispite hem thoghte yt did hem goode
> To synge of hym, and in hire songe dispise
> The foule cherle, that for his coveytise
> Had hem betrayed with his sophistrye
> This was hire songe, 'The foweler we deffye,
> And al his crafte'   And somme songen clere
> Layes of love, that joy it was to here,
> In worshippyng and preysing of hire make;
> And for the newe blisful somere's sake,
> Upon the braunches ful of blosmes softe,
> In hire delyt, they turned hem ful ofte,
> And songen 'Blessed be seynt Valentyne!
> For on his day I chees you to be myne,
> Withouten repentyng, myn herte swete!'"

In one the smooth, even flow of a pensive willowy stream, in the other the rippling animation of a running brook. The difference is radical. But now let us try to get at Mr. Morris's method in dealing with particular scenes   No one can help seeing that he is a very careful and minute observer, and very skillful and patient in the use of his materials, and no one, it seems to us, turning from Chaucer to Mr. Morris, can help seeing also that while Chaucer's way is to make his pictures serve chiefly for illustrations of his text, it is Mr Morris's tendency to make pictures for the picture's sake. Not that Chaucer does not indulge in long descriptions, as in his account of the temples in the Knight's Tale. and dwell upon minute particulars, as in his descriptions of the pilgrims in the Prologue; but in such cases it is his habit mainly to bring forward and insist upon such details only as are significant of the persons and things which he wishes us to see, and help to interpret them to us His Yeoman has a nut head, his Ploughman rides upon a mare, his Monk has a bald head which shines like glass; his Prioress has a straight nose, gray eyes, and a little mouth, she leaves not a bit of grease to be seen on her cup after she has drunk, and is very seemly in her way of reaching after food, his Squire is embroidered like a flowery mead, and so on; all these particulars are vital and to the point Now compare with any of Chaucer's descriptions of men and women Mr Morris's Take one of the best, the beautiful first description of Gudrun Here are details in abundance, hair, eyes, cheeks, brow, bosom, hands, lips, chin, neck, dress, all these are mentioned, and yet after all what do we know about Gudrun, except that she was a beautiful young girl? When Chaucer wishes to tell us no more than that he says, "Emilie the brighte," or

> "Emelie that fairer was to seene
> Than is the lilie on hire stalkes grene,
> And fresscher than the May with flowres newe"

And now turn to Mr. Morris's description of houses and gardens and temples, there are several of them. Read the elaborate description of the Gardens of the Hesperides, in the XIVth Book of Jason: the description of the house in the "Cupid and Psyche," and that in the "Lady of the Land," and others, and notice what a fondness he has for the accumulation of details He loves to enumerate He has a Pre-raphaelite's longing to give everything—everything external In his first book, the "Defence of Guenevere and other Poems," this tendency of his may be seen exercising itself almost without restraint.*

> "Many scarlet bricks there were
> In its walls, and old grey stone,
> Over which red apples shone
> At the right time of the year
>
> On the bricks the green moss grew,
> Yellow lichen on the stone,
> Over which red apples shone,
> Little war that castle knew.
>
> Deep green water filled the moat,
> Each side had a red brick lip,
> Green and mossy with the drip
> Of dew and rain, there was a boat
>
> Of carven wood, with hangings green
> About the stern, it was great bliss
> For lovers to sit there and kiss
> In the hot summer noons, not seen"
>
> "White swans on the green moat
> Small feathers left afloat
> By the blue painted boat,
> Swift running of the stoat,
> Sweet gurgling note by note
> Of sweet music"†

"The Praise of my Lady" is too long to quote; but his lady's hair, her forehead, her eyelids, her eyelashes, her eyes, her chin, her neck, her slim body, her long hands, have each a

---

* With an abandonment indeed, which has in it something so willful that the book seems full of such airs and attitudes and affectations as strike one with amazement, and is as hard reading almost as a 13th Century metrical romance

† In some of this early work it is curious to see what a disposition there is to distinguish things by their colors, rather than by their forms even, or by any inherent qualities, "I sit on a purple bed, outside the wall is red," "The red-billed moor-hen;" scarlet shoon, red lips, gold hair, red-gold hair, gown of white and red, green covered bosoms, &c, and in "The Tomb of King Arthur," Night is the extinguisher of colors, and Twilight the changer of them

> "Upon my red robe, strange in the twilight
> With many unnamed colours"—
> ——"there were no colours then
> For near an hour, and I fell asleep,"
> ——"so that the sun
> Had only just arisen from the deep
> Still land of colours."

separate mention, and after eighteen stanzas about these, hear the nineteenth and the first line of the twentieth:—

> "God pity me though, if I missed
> The telling, how along her wrist
> The veins creep, dying languidly
> Beata mea Domina
> Inside her tender palm and thin"

That is the bent, to miss nothing that the eye can take in as it slowly, pensively passes, without passion either of joy or grief, from object to object, liking one apparently as much as another, and enumerating all. To such a mood and such a method as this Chaucer's straightforward and various style is a thing alien and unattainable. And though from the "Defence of Guenevere" to the "Earthly Paradise," the distance is immense, yet the last work is animated by the same artistic spirit as the first, only corrected, trained, and furnished. But now let us have a specimen of this later work. Here is a picture which one cannot help admiring, in which one can take pleasure again and again.

> "Most fair to peaceful heart was all,
> Windless the ripe fruit down did fall,
> The shadows of the large grey leaves
> Lay grey upon the oaten sheaves
> By the garth-wall as he passed by,
> The startled ousel cock did cry
> As from the yew-tree by the gate
> He flew, the speckled hen did wait
> With outstretched neck his coming in,
> The March-hatched cockerel gaunt and thin
> Crowed shrilly, while his elder thrust
> His stiff wing-feathers in the dust
> That grew aweary of the sun
> The old and one-eyed cart-horse dun.
> The middenstead went hobbling round
> Blowing the light straw from the ground
> With curious eye the drake peered in
> O'er the barn's dusk, where dust and din
> Were silent now a little space"

And now after this take one more, the last, quotation from Chaucer, his description of Chaunteclere:—

> "He loketh as it were a grim lioun,
> And on his toon he rometh up and down,
> Him deyneth not to set his foot to grounde

> He chukkith, whan he hath a corn ifounde,
> And to him rennen than his wifēs alle "

In what we have had to say of Mr. Morris's relation to Chaucer, it has not been our intention to make any closer comparison between them than was immediately necessary to the purpose of illustrating, in a general way, what was meant by the assertion that two poets differing so widely in spirit, could not be like each other in poetic expression, even when dealing with similar materials and endeavoring to produce a similar result For this purpose it was unnecessary to take account of much more in the writings of either than of those portions, and of but a few of those, in which it seemed likely that they would resemble each other, if in any, those namely in which the chief object of either poet was to describe. But it is time to go further in Mr. Morris's case and try to get a less imperfect notion of his position as a poet. We know pretty well already what his aim is as an artist, and under what conditions, either chosen by himself or imposed upon him by necessity, he has undertaken to do his work. If we could be satisfied to ask only, what has the poet attempted, and, on the whole, how has he succeeded in his attempt, it would be enough to speak in general terms of the result, and say no more. But in the case of any considerable work it is impossible to stop there. We need to know more about the work itself, its character and relative position, we want to ask—if voluntarily chosen, was it wise to choose such an aim and to accept such limitations? Or, if imposed upon the poet by necessity, it remains to consider their effect upon his work

The chief limitations of Mr. Morris's work are imposed upon it by his philosophy, and his philosophy is the expression of his temperament. And though one may be pardoned, perhaps, for sometimes wondering, if there may not be a very little affectation in so complete an abandonment to the conditions of such a philosophy; still it is so evident upon the whole, that it is the best fitted to the peculiar temperament and needs of Mr. Morris as an artist, that it will hardly be so well worth while to discuss the wisdom of his acceptance of it, as to consider the effects of it upon his work.

From even so partial an examination as has been made already of his poetry, it has resulted, that a good deal has been said and implied about his ideas on art and nature, and it is plain enough that Mr. Morris has little or no practical sympathy with any theories which represent it as their chief aim and peculiar glory to refer to something beyond themselves. On Mr Morris, nature never makes such an impression as she does on Wordsworth, for example, or on Shelley, nor to him does the aspiration of the artist appear the same thing that it does to Mr. Browning. His is a philosophy that encourages no reference to anything beyond and is unwilling to inquire, and in him, therefore, the love of nature is the love of her outward beauty, and the aim of the artist to minister to an ephemeral pleasure or console a transitory grief. Other poets have thought it enough for them often to ask no more of nature than the pleasure of the present sight, but none of them, not Chaucer, nor Wordsworth, nor Keats, nor Scott, nor Byron, seem ever able to avoid the intrusion of an emotion—communicating itself to the verse—which is strange to Mr Morris, and for none of these—not even Wordsworth or Scott with all their fondness for details—was it ever possible to remain so long contented with the comparatively inferior portions of a landscape as Mr Morris. Scott, in some points of artistic intention the most like to Mr Morris of any of them, without seeking anything beyond the joy of the moment, will thrill with delight when Mr Morris feels only a pensive pleasure; and, while he loves the garden and the flowers of the meadow, loves better the mountain brook and the wild flowers of the hills, and prefers the sunset to the twilight, and the daybreak to the afternoon. But in all these men there was an instinctive love of freedom undreamt of in Mr Morris's philosophy, and another love of life and the beauty of life, than that which moves the tears of the dwellers in the Earthly Paradise.

And yet, if to such pleasure as the freer and more active and more inquiring spirits seek out and find for us in nature, Mr Morris has little or nothing of the same kind to contribute, still to him also, many things have been revealed; things which less patient eyes than his would never have remarked, and which more eager natures could never have obtained. And, in the midst of our regret that his range should be so limited, it is impossible not to see that after all it is under and because of these very limitations that he has been enabled to do some of his best work. As in the dreamy hero of the "Land East of the Sun," his inability to do some things that we wish he could, is his power to do some others that no one else can do. With more passion, with more earnestness, with a wider view and a deeper insight, with greater intellectual force and larger sympathies, he would have been a greater poet, but his most characteristic work would probably never have been done. Wordsworth with as attentive a gaze, and even a keener eye than Mr. Morris for the minutest details of the landscape, was too much engaged in trying to get at the heart of things, too sensitively conscious of the life of the things about him, to be often at liberty to look at them and describe them as if they were mere pictures. But Mr. Morris has the painter's eye. To him things are as parts of pictures, and made to be painted. Where Wordsworth notices that "every flower enjoys the air it breathes," Mr. Morris remarks that it is small and as "red as blood," or that it "flames" in "grey light," or that it has a black or a yellow centre and takes a certain curve in bending. To know such facts as these about flowers, and similar facts about all natural objects, is of more importance to his purpose than to be impressed with a belief that they are alive and enjoying the life they feel, and to the observation and report of such facts as these, accordingly it is his instinct and his habit to confine himself. The range is narrower, of course. Of what Matthew Arnold calls "the grand power of poetry, its interpratıve power," there will be little if any manifestation, but of its pictorial power, its power of naming and arranging the details of a scene so as to bring its outward appearance like a picture before the mind of the reader, of this power there will be many remarkable examples. In fact it is in the exercise of this power that Mr. Morris excels, excelling because, in the first place, as we have just said, it is his instinct to see things rather as pictures or as parts of pictures than as if they were alive and conscious of their life, and, in the second place, because it is possible for him with his temperament, to be a deliberate and accurate observer of details, little disturbed by a conciousness of anything more in what he sees than can be apprehended by the senses, and unvexed by any longing to suggest much more in his descriptions than the very things themselves which he describes. Thus it is that he makes his limitations serve him; what he describes he seems to have seen, and his best descriptions make very nearly the same impression on us as if we had stood before a painting of an actual scene, and been enabled easily, quietly, and at leisure to look at each separate object, passing lightly from this to that, sometimes tempted to linger, but never forced to try to "see into the life of things," or stand surprised before

> 'A presence that disturbs us with the joy
> Of elevated thoughts'

How well such a kind of pictorial description is adapted to some of Mr Morris's needs, as a teller of tales, pure and simple, need not be said. To read "The Man Born to be King," is almost like taking the walks and rides that the persons of the story take, going on with them from place to place, talking little, thinking little, doing little, but seeing many things, among others such a scene as this:

> ' Then downward he began to wend,
> And 'twixt the flowery hedges sweet
> He heard the hook smite down the wheat,
> And murmur of the unseen folk,
> And when he reached the stream that broke
> The golden plain, but leisurely
> He passed the bridge, for he could see
> The masters of that ripening realm,
> Cast down beneath an ancient elm
> Upon a little strip of grass
> From hand to hand the pitcher pass,
> While on the turf beside them lay
> The ashen-handled sickles grey,
> The matters of their cheer between·
> Slices of white cheese, specked with green,
> And greenstriped onions and ryebread,
> And summer apples faintly red
> Even beneath the crimson skin;
> And yellow grapes well ripe and thin,
> Plucked from the cottage gable-end "

This is not seeing things deeply, but it is seeing them with surprising accuracy and clearness. He seems to fix his eye exactly upon the objects which he wishes us to notice, and to resign himself without reserve to the simple, single task of reporting faithfully what he sees and no more. The verse omits to be musical, but it pictures like a glassy pool, even to the green specks in the white cheese, and the stripes upon the onions; and that is what Mr. Morris meant that it should do; that is what Mr Morris means that the greater portion of his poetry shall chiefly do, it shall make pictures. Even his songs do it, the interpolated songs in the "Earthly Paradise" are almost all descriptions, and here is a song that Orpheus sings in contention with the Sirens.—

> "O the sweet valley of deep grass
> Wherethrough the summer stream doth pass,
> In chain of shadow, and still pool,
> From misty morn to evening cool,
> Where the black ivy creeps and twines
> O'er the dark-armed, red-trunked pines,
> Whence clattering the pigeon flits,
> Or, brooding o er her thin eggs, sits,
> And every hollow of the hills
> With echoing song the mavis fills
> There by the stream, all unafraid
> Shall stand the happy shepherd maid,
> Alone in first of sunlit hours,
> Behind her, on the dewy flowers,
> Her homespun woolen raiment lies,
> And her white limbs and sweet grey eyes
> Shine from the calm green pool and deep,
> While round about the swallows sweep,
> Not silent, and would God that we
> Like them, were landed from the sea."

So strong is this tendency in him, and so great a part of his genius is it, that he cannot be satisfied to let us imagine a thing for ourselves; he sees what he describes and will make us see it as he sees it. He sees even in his dreams, his "eyes make pictures when they are shut." Even his monsters, his dragons, his chimaera have all their share of description, and where he so far restrains himself as to confuse the outline, he still cannot resist the temptation to color them with care, or to indulge in some such detail about them as makes it plain that the things are conceived of by him as objects to be seen and not merely to be felt. And as for faeries, and gods, and goddesses, he looks at them generally as if they were men and women, and draws, and drapes and colors them as such. And see how he realizes the ghostly procession in the latter part of "The Ring Given to Venus," deliberately describing, as if from actual sight, shape after shape as it passes by, till he comes to the "Lord of all".

> "Most like a mighty king was he,
> And crowned and sceptred royally;
> As a white flame his visage shone,
> Sharp, clear-cut as a face of stone,
> But flickering flame, not flesh it was,
> And over it such looks did pass
> Of wild desire, and pain, and fear,
> As in his people's faces were,
> But tenfold fiercer, furthermore,
> A wondrous steed the Master bore,
> Unnameable of kind or make,
> Not horse, nor hippogriff, nor drake,
> Like and unlike to all of these"

And his men and women he sees as pictures, and like to pictures

> "But with him was a boy, right fair
> Grey-eyed and yellow haired, most like
> Unto some Michael who doth strike
> The dragon on a minster-wall,
> So sweet-eyed was he and withal
> So fearless of all things he seemed"

Gudrun's first appearance is as a complete picture in a frame, and here is Cydippe among the tulips:

> "And his heart stopped awhile for there
> Against a flowering thorn-bush fair,
> Hidden by tulips to the knee,
> His heart's desire his eyes did see,
> Clad was she e'en as in the dove
> Who makes the summer sad with love,
> High girded as one hastening
> In swift search for some longed-for thing;
> Her hair drawn by a silken band
> From her white neck, and in her hand
> A myrtle-spray"

And to him their actions even are as pictures. His description —in "The Ring Given to Venus"—of the games in the garden is a picture of astonishing distinctness, and indeed, "lovely to look on :"

> "Lovely to look on was the sway
> Of the slim maidens 'neath the hall
> As they swung back to note its fall
> With dainty balanced feet; and fair
> The bright outflowing golden hair,
> As swiftly, yet in measured wise
> One maid ran forth to gain the prize;
> Eyes glittered and young cheeks glowed bright,
> And gold-shod foot, round limb and light,
> Gleamed from beneath the girded gown
> That, unrebuked, untouched, was thrown
> Hither and thither by the breeze"

> "There others on the daisies lay
> Above the moat and watched their quill
> Make circles in the water still,
> Or laughed to see the damsel hold
> Her dainty skirt enwrought with gold
> Back from the flapping tench's tail,
> Or to his close-set dusky mail
> With gentle force brought laughingly
> The shrinking finger tip anigh"

This is charming, and an excellent specimen of the wonderful things that can be effected within the limits of the pictorial style. And now as a general illustration of Mr. Morris's dominant tendency, note finally how fond all his women and goddesses are of contemplating their own beauty; how they are always lifting their long skirts when they move, and letting them fall when they stop, what a loosening and letting down there is of long gold hair, what a putting on and putting off of raiment; what a fluttering of gowns, and what a clinging of them to slim bodies and round limbs. His painter's eye seems never to have enough of these appearances But for us, remembering how frequent they are in his poems, we begin to feel the pressure of the limitations and to ask ourselves if this fondness for the outside of things is not excessive, if there is not a little too much "pointing out," if things are not often made a little too plain to us, and if we are not forced often to see some things which we would rather feel; if, in short, Mr. Morris in so bountifully providing for the senses is not in danger of cloying the appetite he feeds And withal there is so very little bread to all this immeasurable deal of nectar. There is as little plain living as high thinking, as little sensuality as spirituality; it is all sensuousness. And certainly it is curious to notice, with all Mr. Morris's realism, how little reality we get after all. He pictures things to us so effectually, that we cease to care for them except as pictures, and his men and women become little more than pictures and statues, pleasant to the eye, but little dear to the heart. In even the poems that have the most of humanity in them, in which he attempts to answer the inevitable demand for a more continuous recognition and fuller treatment of human interests—the Jason—the Gudrun—the two Bellerophons—he still, it seems to us, relies too much upon the picture-making method, and from lack of concentration and speed, and from want of penetrative power, fails to interest us deeply in Medea, and Gudrun, and Bellerophon themselves, and with all his skill, is unable to give the characters individual force and life enough, to make Bellerophon seem to differ much from Perseus, or Medea from Gudrun. In fact, "the human heart by which we live," is not Mr Morris's first consideration, for he really, we think, cares very little for actual men and women, and is constitutionally rather shy of them than otherwise. But certain of its joys and sorrows he sympathises with, and some of its tendernesses, he can represent with a peculiar grace. Indeed, to us, one of the most interesting things to notice in Mr Morris's work, is the connection that exists between his fondness for the outside of things, his liking to see clearly and accurately what he paints, and to paint little else than he can see; and his natural choice of what emotions he shall deal with, and of the manner in which he shall treat of them. The one tendency is the legitimate offspring of the other. For such emotions and such moods of mind as have their birth and abode in the debateable land between the possible and the impossible, between sleeping and waking, Mr Morris has a regard which seems like fascination. Devoted to things visible, and striving to fix his attention on these, and not to slip off and go beyond the object itself, practically believing that it is useless to try to go beyond it. it follows of course, that whatever he cannot clearly apprehend, whatever is doubtful, and obscure, and mysterious in nature and human life, disturbs and pains him more or less. He cannot help seeing and feeling that there are secrets, but he cannot and will not attempt to discover and possess them; he takes no pleasure in speculating about them; where he cannot see, he will not venture far, all beyond, is to him an unknown country, which affects him somewhat, if one may say so, as darkness affects children. The result is, that for the representation of moods of unending reverie and states of dreamy half-consciousness, and for the expression of such visionary fears and nameless dreads, such sudden and inexplicable sinkings of the heart, such vague regrets and inefficient longings, such strange emotions of self-pity and the like as are natural to those who are fond of things clear and simple, and hence sensitive to things obscure and complicated, for the representation and expression of these he has a peculiar aptitude and ability. Hatred and dread of death, not knowing what it means, except that it is an end of life and its pleasures had or hoped for, and love of life for the mere life's sake, this, it is unnecessary to say, is the prevailing sentiment which he never lets us lose sight of from the beginning of the Jason to the end of the Earthly Paradise. And with this too goes a conviction of the vanity of all things done or attempted, seldom so fully expressed in any poetry, and probably never in so even a tone of quiet, helpless, merely pensive melancholy; and a vague, vain, passive pity for the sum of human suffering, so vague and vain as apparently never to feel any need of the relief of indignation or of the consolation of hope. There is no desperate cursing of the gods, no passionate hoping against hope, "till hope creates, from its own wreck, the thing it contemplates," the acquiescence is complete, and the pity that results little more than the self-pity of pleasure-loving natures devoid of will, and incapable of despair. See what an utter abandonment to the most self-regarding and most incapable melancholy there is in such a passage as this:

> "Sirs, ye are old, and ye have seen perchance
> Some little child for very gladness dance
> Over a scarcely-noticed worthless thing,
> Worth more to him than ransom of a king,
> Did not a pang of more than pity take
> Your heart therent, not for the youngling's sake,

> But for your own, for man that passes by,
> So like to God, so like the beasts that die —
> Lo sirs, my pity for myself is such
> When like an image that my hand can touch
> My old self grows unto myself grown old.'*

This is fine in its way, but a deeper pathos is in the timid question, that John's old mother asks him tearfully after his return from Faeryland

> "Fair art thou come again, sweet son,
> And sure a long way hast thou gone
> I durst not ask thee where; but this
> I ask thee by the first sweet kiss,
> Wherewith I kissed thy new-born face
> Long since within the groaning place—
> If thou hast been so far, that thou
> Canst tell to me—grown old, son, now,
> Through weary life, unsatisfied
> Desires, and lingering hope untried—
> If thou canst tell me of thy ruth,
> What thing there is of lies or truth,
> In what the new faith saith of those
> Great glories of the heavenly close,
> And how that poor folk twinned on earth
> Shall meet therein in joy and mirth"

Indeed, this whole story of "The Land East of the Sun,"—to us, in spite of its diffuseness and its too great length, one of the most suggestive and winning of all his poems—is full of examples of a very delicate perception of the unacknowledged fears, the incommunicable doubts of one's own identity, the indefinable longings, and strange regrets, the bewilderment and loneliness, and all the shadowy emotions that haunt the borderland of sleep, to which we have already alluded. The mixture of forgetfulness and memory, the loneliness and the yearning for more human companionship that clouds John's bliss in Faeryland; the confusion of mind, the feeling of estrangement

---

* Compare his "Master," Chaucer's noble and affecting lines
> "That thee ys sent receyve in buxomnesse,
> The wrasteling of this world asketh a falle,
> Her is no home, her is but wyldyrnesse
> Forth pilgrimé! forth, best out of thy stalle!
> Loke up on hye, and thanke God of alle,
> Weyve thy lust, and let thy goste thee lede,
> And trouthe shal thee delyver, hit is no drede"

that comes over him on his return to his kinsfolk and his father's farm, the "shame at not being of them," the unshared longing, the lonely melancholy, the miserable doubt, the numbing sense of repression, the heavy languor and all the death in life of hopeless but inevitable love that wastes him after his return, and makes him feel "himself as in a cage shown to the gaping world;" these, and the experiences of the journey, and the strange grief and joy of the final meeting; all these are beautifully represented, and with a sympathetic insight into the "blank misgivings of a creature, moving about in worlds unrealized," that makes one wonder again if Mr. Morris is not doing himself a wrong in submitting so loyally to the conditions of his philosophy.

But he submits; even in love he will not attempt to force the barriers, he will not aspire. The greater part of his poetry is about love, but it is very nearly all the same. It is the chief pleasure of the "Earthly Paradise,' but, like all its other pleasures, sensuous for the most part; a love that comes in at the eye and goes very little deeper, never coarse, seldom heartily sensual even, in spite of its overfondness for the body, for its color, and smoothness, and suppleness, and grace; never really passionate, in spite of its flushings, and palings, and languors, and longings, never enthusiastic, never in a rapture, never out of itself. Little more generally than a languid, dreamy, self-conscious voluptuousness, wise enough always to mix a little pain with pleasure, that loves to lie and look at Amaryllis in the shade, and play with Neaera's fingers and the tangles of her hair, and sigh "twixt kiss and kiss," as it thinks a little of quick coming death or inevitable change. It is the love of the body,

"Lips like a scarlet thread, skin lily-white,
Round chin, smooth brow 'neath the dark hair's delight,
Fair neck, slim hands, and dainty limbs, well hid,"

and depends upon the body; Cupid would not get from Father Jove this grace for Psyche,

"That she should never die, but her sweet face
And wonderful fair body should endure,"

a love of the present;

"Love while ye may; if twain grow into one
'Tis for a little while; the time goes by"

that fears to look upon the future,

"I love thee so, I think upon the end'

a love whose ideal is, exempt from death and change, to live forever in a sweet forgetfulness of all the troubles of the world and all its fears, prolonging love's first day to all eternity There is humanity in this certainly. But so sadly fond is Mr. Morris of brooding over the inevitable nature of death and change, and so much and yet so little does he value life and love, that he cannot resist the temptation, in season and out of season, here, there and everywhere of impressing his favorite belief upon us, even to satiety At first it is pleasant enough to see two lovers, waked up for the first time to a quick consciousness of the value of life and time, glow shudderingly aware of the possibility of death and change, and "weep to have that which they fear to lose;" and in Shakespeare's sonnet and in Mr Morris's "How can I have enough of life and love, the thought comes home to us as natural and appropriate But Mr Morris is continually going further, and filling the whole atmosphere of love with such a scent of mortality and such sighs of self-pity, and tears of voluptuous pain, that it becomes heavy and hard to breathe It is a mistake in art if nothing more, it is too frequent and too obtrusive, it fails of its intended effect and becomes part of the too much that helps the poems to some of their monotony There is a dramatic propriety in Medea's forebodings as she leaves her father's palace, but consider the case of Andromeda, whose love, so far as we know, was happy to the end To us it seems that the beauty of the first part of the love scene is considerably lessened by the unneeded melancholy of its ending.

"There on a rock smoothed by the washing sea
They sat, and eyed each other lovingly
And few words at the first the maiden said,
So wrapped she was in all the goodlihead
Of her new life made doubly happy now
For her alone the sea-breeze seemed to blow,
For her in music did the white surf fall,
For her alone the wheeling birds did call
Over the shallows, and the sky for her
Was set with white clouds, far away and clear,
E'en as her love, this strong and lovely one,
Who held her hand, was but for her alone"

This is beautiful. But when Andromeda says afterward,

> "O love, to think that love can pass away,
> That soon or late, to us shall come a day
> When this shall be forgotten! e'en this kiss
> That makes us now forget the high God's bliss,
> And sons of men with all their miseries,"

is it not a little overmuch for Mr. Morris to make Perseus answer in such words as these

> "And if thou needs must think of that dull night
> That creepeth on no otherwise than this,
> Yet for that thought hold closer to thy bliss,
> Come nigher, come! forget the more they pain"

If this be a reproduction of Greek sentiment, if these be the manners of the early world,* O, how much good a little of Chaucer's "frank anachronism" would have done Mr. Morris!† And how much too, a little of Byron's passion would have helped to reconcile us to this worship of the body! Let any one compare Mr. Morris's love-makings with one that this scene with Andromeda partly resembles, the magnificent love-scene between Juan and Haidee, in the second canto of the "Don Juan," and see the difference between describing a thing as if it had been seen as a picture, and describing it as if it had been seen as an event In Mr. Morris's pictures, his persons take graceful attitudes and are beautifully draped and colored, but they seem as if fixed in position, there is no progression in

---

* Of the manners of the past, especially as shown in its art—Grecian, and of the Middle Age—Mr. Morris has evidently a good deal of knowledge And he would like apparently to keep more or less close to the time of his story In the "Defence of Guenevere, etc ," he becomes almost pedantic in his treatment of some subjects drawn from the times of the Black Prince In his later poems, however, he wisely allows himself greater freedom, though still intending to be generally true to the manners of the age with which he has to do But he is truer, we think, to his own nature,—as indeed he should be, for that matter,—as an artist, and as he cannot help being, as a genuine part really of the 19th century, with all his preference for the past. And hence, though there may be and is a certain amount of truth to Grecian sentiment (one side of it) in his versions of the Grecian stories, the prevailing sentiment, we think, belongs, and is to be criticised as belonging, not so much to the Greek astto the Dream-World of Mr Morris, and to Mr Morris himself

† Chaucer makes Troilus, like a mediæval knight, talk of his unworthiness, and his hope of being made a nobler and better man through virtue of his love for Cressida.

Lightning Source UK Ltd.
Milton Keynes UK
UKHW020740200722
406119UK00005B/543